Cover art by Mahima Golani

attachment

Eliette Chanezon

To Simon for the joy of language, in all possible shapes,
To Charlotte for nineteen years of noticing the small details,
To Papa for the love of poetry, and for Baudelaire,
To Maman for thinking in bright colors and teaching us that love is too large to ever be defined,
To Mahima for letting me bask in your metaphorical mind,
To Marinca for showing me to the music of language,
To Alizée for countless readings, rereadings, rerereadings,
To Gabby for being the first and the forever,
To Mrs. Capur for showing me poetry as a language not a rhyme scheme,
To Farah, Tanishka, Steph, Cara, Beatrix, Rosalie for all of the images and for letting me experience your brilliant associative minds,
To Solange, Ansley, Samuel, Milton for the sharing, the questioning, the constant inspiration,
To Léa, Ema, Ana, Lani, Shaida, Sara, Meena, Maggie, Hanish, Jissa for a kind of love and support without which this book wouldn't have come to be,

Thank you, thank you, thank you.

Table of contents

I p. 12

Anesthetics
Aurore
Park benches
Delancey/Essex
The ABC of desire
Baudelaire
Hospital bed (1)

II p. 19

Les dents du bonheur
Little L
To be scared of oneself
Moon shadows
Blemished
Réveil
Mahima
Hospital bed (2)

III p. 29

Rêve
Cliffhanger
Eyelashes
My favorite tree
Les papillons
Hospital bed (3)

IV p. 37

Dusk
The 7pm swing
Blackberries
Hippocampus
Dollar slices
Hospital bed (4)

V p. 45

Marilyn (1)
To watch a loved one cry
Banana ice
Jealousy
Marilyn (2)
Ikea
Unladylike

VI p. 57

Coffee will taste the same tomorrow
Intermission
Bushwick
Smile lines
A waltz and a half
In Marvin's room

VII p. 64

Désamour
Efflorescence
ερωτας
Bathroom sink
Digitus III
Bedside
Gargoyles
Crimson
Sometimes I wonder if longing is a prerequisite for good poetry
Top notch

8

I
attachment is a lightbulb hanging from a ceiling
a safety hazard
but how soft it makes a room

Anesthetics

for the first time in a long time
the sun set and it was just a sunset
poetry has left the brown rooftops
now a stone is a stone

days move through you
one by one and all the same

insides of your cheeks lacquered
in bodega coffee and borrowed cigarettes
you never knew it'd be so nice
to feel nothing at all

Aurore

every morning, dawn raises
a periwinkle eyebrow
over ass grabs and 2-dollar bouquets

pride
a new york summer sweat
sand under fingernails
we let go of it

Park benches

strangers who sit
on chipped park benches
etch memories into tired wood
with the graze of a palm

jaded but still dreaming
always, and harder every day
of tenderness past

sometimes I wish a flower was a flower for its petals and its
stems
a cup of coffee just a cup for its handle and its rim
silence merely silence
and benches only benches
relieved of everybody's yesterdays

Delancey/Essex

a shoulder in a trench coat
he reminds me of
water, rippleless
unbearably unbothered
and more beautiful still

The ABC of desire

A

for Helvetica

because when the sun comes up so do my morals
a clean nod when I walk past you
clean like click and swoosh and sharp-cut Helvetica

B

for inbox

because I craft a sterile sentence
your name in the address bar,
followed by the remembrance of the same
pointed syllables, stretching the barrel
of a gun put on mute

C

for a one-way ticket to the small of my back

because I crave things I cannot have

-

This is a thought for the Unsent

because Eve was pushed onto Adam
when all she wanted was the fruit

because I wonder which women have unraveled you

because how is it
that I see a mountain and
you know a pebble

Baudelaire

Think upon me in your photographic mind's eye
like Baudelaire thinks upon the women
whose bodies he writes in rhymes

Hospital bed (1)

in the sixth month you lost the last beads of hope
and let one cell melt every limb
tissue paper soft

II
attachment is a dusty ray of sun
passing through stained glass
it's wanting to be held but not touched

Les dents du bonheur

it's the afternoon
on the carpet

there's a space between your two front teeth
we call it les dents du bonheur
happiness teeth

winter fog slides down the window
your happiness teeth smile in my ear
we're on the carpet and I'm falling in love

Little L

I don't know if I believe in Love with a capital L

but here is a cup of black coffee, hot even in the summertime
a pile of folded clothes
a pinky finger hold

here is a book, swollen from sand and salt water
here are my lips, swollen from kisses and too much sun

I believe in a million world-stopping moments
and hope for lifetimes of love in lowercase

To be scared of oneself

It sounds like shuffling hands
looks like the underside of a pillow
and appears only when
to be a woman feels like a cut

Moon shadows

un petit pli
tracé au pinceau

I can see it when I open my eyes

un petit pli
très appliqué

on window lit train rides
foggy-morning bright
I hold that little fold wrapped
around my frontal lobe

I can see it when I close my eyes

wrapped, the way my fingers hook
around your shoulders

sheets soaked in shower water
I lay with moonlight in my chest
full of Eskimo kisses
of your lowered eyelids
full to the brim

un petit pli
pour un si grand sourire
à 600 kilomètres
que j'aimerais toucher

Blemished

overnight a little field
one hydrangea, one peony, two blue lilies
grew into a secret
for this turtleneck to keep

Réveil

Le premier nuage
aux contours engourdis par la nuit
attend, les joues couleur groseille,
dans les coulisses du matin.

Mahima

love
in a laugh wet still from crying
in lips and eyes and knuckles and knees
is what makes a room a home

it rests on the side of the bathtub
that I sit on when she bathes
and it spreads like the two clouds of milk
that she takes in her tea

Hospital bed (2)

In the fourth month you did your braids
in bathroom mirrors
happily pathetic
or wishing to be seen.
When the leaves fell so did your hair
your head was bare
summer peach soft
you said at least there's no split ends.

III
attachment is being put on hold
and staying on the line

Rêve

Last night, ridiculously
alone between four darkened walls
two duvet covers
her hands become your hands
and the very best part
is no one has to know

Cliffhanger

the wind went from screaming, to singing, to silence
night swallowed the desert whole

I sat with soil under my feet
when shame let go of me the way
heat lets go of the rock at night
leaving it stark, barren, indiscernible

in the dark something emerged

a morsel of hope, naked
wiped clean from remorse and longing
that one day you would sit with me again
under a star-dotted sky

un petit bout d'espoir
durci par le temps et le silence
que je m'étais caché

eyelashes

two hundred pencil strokes
a calligraphy frame
hanging, lowered
over a painting of the world
that I wish I could see

My favorite tree

it lives on Poinsettia and Fountain ave
a prunus with big arms
thorny clavicles
it sheds blossoms the way
stories leave our bodies
one by one
sinewing down
so that everyone stands in a little puddle
of their own fallen blossoms

les papillons

I pasted a daydream right where I could find it
it sits on the corner of Frederick and Cole
it's where I catch myself smiling alone

Hospital bed (3)

she used to roll her Rs

her hips

her own cigarettes

in the third month it was her veins

that rolled

for every stuck needle

on the ceiling then
was a patch of brown light
cast by her gaze

IV
attachment is a touch of orange
in an impressionist's sunrise
too dim a sight to survive
for longer than a blink

Dusk

is a marlboro gold, escaping
in grey ribbons
to braid itself with fog
and up the eucalyptus trees

addicted to leaving
cautious and unashamed
and blurring all the tracks

The 7pm swing

The trombonist
moments before his last solo
pictures blowing himself right into the trombone
one robust breath and he's
dancing inside of it
shiny shoes against brass floors

you could be this trombonist
swaying in a body
that belongs only to you

unbothered, romantic,
soaked in orange light and mosquito bites
you could find solace in a hot sunset
wet hair
or in the way a flower folds.

Blackberries

Sometimes my fear comes undone
careless rash and selfish

like dark drupelets off a blackberry
collected in the palm of a hand

I try to memorize your face
as if I know what's coming

And as if even if I did
I could reason it all away

Hippocampus

like an icy bough on a snowy morning
to frost upon a touch
disarmed by the sight
of the first light hitting your clavicles

to use this moment
extend the seconds
store your gaze in a week-long box of memories
to replay on bus-rides and runs to the beach

to feel the way the dust might feel
when light turns it into glitter

Dollar slices

with lips covered
in carmex and compliments
take a bite straight from the throat
knowing how
right at the Adam's apple

Hospital bed (4)

In the last month there's room enough
for two times ten toes at the foot of the bed.

Blue sheet, blue eyes, blue man
built like something to hold onto.

Bars of light from the half open blinds
land on his cheek while he sleeps
like the folds she once loved
the ones left by the sheets.

Two tucked rag dolls in room 36
still in blue
still in love
(maybe)

V
attachment is Icarus flying toward the Sun
freeing yourself slowly
and falling back open

Marilyn

it feels like sickness still
only when I'm alone
like nighttime is a long, hot shower where your mind's eye
gets pruned
imagining the same grin
against another pretty mouth

To watch a loved one cry

someone's made you feel like the hard bits of the steak
the ones people spit out
politely
and leave on the side of their plate
hoping no one saw them do it

I wish I knew how to fix a wound that resides in the body
to wipe away the tears sticking to your chin
like I used to pull at the little bits of dried washable glue on
my notebooks

my love you are more than an enigma
you've got 10 ribbons where other people have toes
you come complete, and big, and real
fully formed

even a Brasserie style deep dish cheesy quiche
can feel like a thick crust slice
drying up in the 24 hour fluorescence of Ray's pizza
when held by the wrong pair of hands

there is elegance in a crippled heart
a crippled heart is a heart that's lived

Banana Ice

puff bar in hand
I thaw away in the bathtub
pruned, pathetic
and yet somehow tougher

feeling my whole body shiver
from the curve of my hoops to poorly painted toes
with the beating, lively, sensation
that to be alone is to be free

Jealousy

it lingers
all new and visceral, bites
like the imaginary amazons
who creep their way
underneath my eyelids
smoothed-skinned
crafted to please

Marilyn (2)
To be blissful

to be looked through the way one looks through a window
shrunken by a gaze so honest
that you wish you could strip it of everything that makes
him brilliant
so you'd have nothing left to wait on

to catch yourself blissful in a darkened phone screen
a grin made of jaeger, coca cola,
and one giddy shot of homemade idiocy

Ikea

Hers was the last missing piece of her grönmalchvelt
bookshelf
probably not needed
but still in the miscellaneous crap plate in the hallway
just in case

Unladylike

at the last, shy, footsteps
of an ending piano piece
things are butter knife dull
and somehow that's better

tonight ladies and gentlemen
under the neon lights
Gershwin presents
rhapsody in fuck you

Johnny James

I've hated someone
a hatred scalding hot
for gifting me their fear
wrapped up nicely in red muslin

but to hate is to remember and all I want is to forget

At every step I am so scared
scared to give scared to receive

Now
as I buy back the neighborhoods and songs and steadfast
step they had stolen from me
street by street, kindness by kindness
conquering the things I'd lost,
I think

Forgiveness is a dish best eaten warm
on a summer plate
with all of the colors of a life well lived
of a faith worth giving
of honesty worth tending to
no matter how hard

love knows only its own lifetime
which was shorter than ours
but bold enough to believe in

I wish you tonight
an embrace so right you may forget for more than an
instant
that you are afraid too

Spring

one day
the folds under their eyes
won't be in the morning's first cup of tea

Hospital bed (last)

Picture her unsinkable
ears submerged
in watercolors, very still

held by the beautiful minute
and all the small grotesque
of the forty-nine years before her heart came loose

beating its way out of its home
and into all of those places
that will never see her.

57

VI
attachment is sleeping with a night light
when I miss you I am not alone

Coffee will taste the same tomorrow

1
woke up last night from a nightmare
yours was the only shape I wanted next to me

there will be others
and they won't be you
and I'll probably wish that they were

until one day it stops feeling
like my heart belongs to you and my body to your hands

2
I wish I could take all of the places that have seen us
together and put them away

3
I'd put songs in the box too, and bibimbap, and crepes, and
so many shows and so many views,
and so many things I hear myself say, mannerisms I see
myself do,
I'd put my whole self in a box because I can't stop thinking
about you

4
everything is harder
harder, and duller

5
your birthday present arrived at my house yesterday
I didn't send it back

Intermission

eyeballs left waiting under eyelids, wanting
the only thing taking my breath away
is a strong cigarette

Bushwick

Ce soir sur la terrasse
l'été doux et puant de Brooklyn au mois d'Août
je me découvre à découvert

À t'aimer comme si c'était une évidence
laisser glisser toutes mes défenses
ne laisser plus

Qu'une table
deux chaises
une brume cendrée
et ton sourire en diagonale

Smile lines

the faces we try to memorize
all turn cloudy after a while

still we keep them close
as if sewn into the crook of our palm
and every new face we hold
blurs the contours of smile lines we've loved

when the familiar disappears
we are naked in our aloneness
it has happened before and will happen again

features give way to gratitude
and longing gives way to hope

A waltz and a half

the time that it takes
to rinse memories off of
the insides of eyelids until
until they're canvas blank
two rolls of film in the light

In Marvin's room

these days my dreams are pumice stone
smooth, rippleless
not much is solid

only a vision
of being loved not harder only better
of being held not tighter only closer

and a hope
that you'll fall for someone much like yourself
with the same kindness
the same full heart
the same cowardice

VII
attachment is New York City through a window
when the neighbor's floor lamp is your only Sun

Désamour

I wrote you down in a notebook
it spat you right out

Efflorescence

Tonight
the You that you find behind the shower curtain
is bare and friable
undone by water
the way
April undresses the orchids
leaving behind fields and fields
of scattered petals

έρωτας

Sunday on the bedspread
hidden from sun and prying eyes
my finger drags across your lips

here
a Cupid's bow

here
two smile lines

and right here
indiscernible
is a little dip

It's an apostrophe
punctuating the side
of this mouth I want to kiss

Ta cheíli mou erotévontai ti voutiá sto mágouló sou

I keep your bold smile
painted inside of my eyelids
hidden
from sun and prying eyes

Ta dáchtylá mou erotévontai tous ómous sou

Sunday on the bedspread
my finger drags across my hips

here
at the top of my thighs

here
where my two legs embrace
is a tiny blue mark

it is mine
and it is yours

it is no one else's

Ta mátia mou erotévontai ta mátia sou

6 thousand kilometers away
I starve for calloused hands on skin
when all I can give you are words

I want to peel mandarins in the grass and eat them with our
hands
to hold you tight in dimly lit ballrooms
salty sea water
downtown summer sweat

so many moments to cut in half
and devour together

so much time to do it

Bathroom sink

Now the back of my throat is covered in flowers
buttercups, hollyhocks, pink lilies.
It's my own name written on the petals
in tentative, cursive letters.

Now I grow shrubs inside of my cheeks
big and bulbous
gorgeous, glaring
in toothpaste-stained mirrors
when I open my mouth.

At night I spit them out
milky marble, soapy hair
and watching them slip down
I feel one grow again

Digitus III

I was six years old when I came to know it,
grounded and cruelly deprived
of raspberry tart for a week
for having brandished it proudly
in the buttery face of a mean kid in school

today in the city of whistlers in cars
I rediscover it
in its abrasive majesty

like Keats to the nightingale, Shelley to the west wind
this is an ode
a sonnet 18 to my middle finger
loyal protector
and most dexterous lover

I raise a tall, proud, middle finger
to the Don Juan knockoff in his Honda Civic
for every raspberry here's my Digitus III

Bedside
got ankles tree trunk thick and
rough like battered boots
"senti, senti, senti", said
in the sandpaper voice of those who sense
themselves leaving
feel, feel, feel

Gargoyles

Too long spent fixed in place
tripping on eagerness and banana peels
turning myself inside out

Wanting more
fumbling at the thought of asking

But hope taints the cheeks of those who have something to
look forward to

Mine are red red poppy red
happiness is in
and my friends move at night
like agile dancers on a canvas

We drink fruit juice
lick tiramisu off our fingertips
find joy in the silly things
talk even when it doesn't matter
(especially when it doesn't matter)

tear ducts gone brittle from being unused
we eat raspberries
laugh loud
and let the clouds erase the rest

Crimson

surprised and emboldened
emboldened by surprise
to find in the mirror
the softened angles of a woman's body

to meet with loving eyes
the slope of my hip
the crest of my chest

a hilly landscape
moving, folding, growing
all mine

Sometimes I wonder if longing is a prerequisite for poetry

For sounds of table setting through a window
soil crackling under bare feet
the breathing of the laundry machine at night

For spots of sunlight on a kitchen floor and tiles of many colors
cricket songs, family breakfasts, grainy sketching paper

Walking home with the handhold of the street lights
And I think, there will never be enough time

Top notch

at nap time I sleep naked
to old school jams
window open
fingertips still coated in smoke

I let myself daydream in great vivid detail
secretly
about things I wouldn't admit to

every year in this garden
we grow taller, greener, dusty
finding new joy and new sadness

all of us dainty flowers
sweet and delicate
with fingers that smell like tobacco tar and acetone
calloused feet and and rude ideas

I used to think independence meant needing no one
I think it's more knowing you are needed too

Made in the USA
Las Vegas, NV
05 September 2023